THE JERSEY DEVIL VS. MOTHMAN

by Golriz Golkar

CAPSTONE PRESS
a capstone imprint

Published by Capstone Press, an imprint of Capstone
1710 Roe Crest Drive, North Mankato, Minnesota 56003
capstonepub.com

Copyright © 2026 by Capstone. All rights reserved. No part of this publication may be reproduced in whole or in part, or stored in a retrieval system, or transmitted in any form or by any means, electronic, mechanical, photocopying, recording, or otherwise, without written permission of the publisher.

Library of Congress Cataloging-in-Publication Data is available on the Library of Congress website.

ISBN: 9798875225680 (hardcover)
ISBN: 9798875225635 (paperback)
ISBN: 9798875225642 (ebook PDF)

Summary: Two red-eyed creatures fly toward each other. One has large bat wings. The other has mothlike wings. They both let out a screech as they attack. It's the Jersey Devil versus Mothman!

Editorial Credits
Editor: Julie Gassman; Designer: Hilary Wacholz; Media Researcher: Rebekah Hubstenberger; Production Specialist: Tori Abraham

Image Credits
Alamy: Matthew Corrigan, 13 (left); Getty Images: iStock/Clara Bastian, 18, iStock/Mubera Boskov, 16; Shutterstock: Daniel Eskridge, cover, 5 (top), 6, 19 (jersey devil), 29 (jersey devil), delcarmat, 7, gnepphoto, 29 (ribbon medal), Hatteviden, 13 (right), JM-MEDIA, 5 (bottom), 11, 15, 20–21, 25, 26, 27, Mimadeo, 9, R. Formidable, 17, SimpleB, 22–23, WinWin artlab, 19 (broken bars)

Design Elements
Getty Images: iStock/AdrianHillman; Shutterstock: Ballerion, Yana Lyso

Any additional websites and resources referenced in this book are not maintained, authorized, or sponsored by Capstone. All product and company names are trademarks™ or registered® trademarks of their respective holders.

Printed and bound in China. 006276

TABLE OF CONTENTS

READY FOR BATTLE 4

THEIR BEGINNINGS 8

SPOOKY CREATURES 12

THE BATTLE BEGINS 24

Glossary 30

Read More .31

Internet Sites 31

Index 32

About the Author 32

Words in **bold** are in the glossary.

READY FOR BATTLE

It is a dark summer night. The Jersey Devil stands tall on its strong **hind** legs. Large bat wings fan out. Its eyes glow red. It screeches loudly.

Suddenly, Mothman appears above. Its mothlike wings flap quickly. Its red eyes grow wide. It lets out a big squeak. It's one **cryptid** against another. Who will win the battle?

Name: The Jersey Devil

Alias: The Leeds Devil

Type of Cryptid: Batlike

Height: 3 to 10 feet (0.9 to 3 meters) tall

Features: Furry body, large bat wings, glowing red eyes, long narrow tail

First Sighting: 1735

Range (Area): New Jersey, Maryland, Pennsylvania, and Delaware

Likes: Animal and **crop** snacks

Dislikes: Humans in its way

Name: Mothman

Alias: None

Type of Cryptid: Humanoid/Mothlike

Height: 6 to 7 feet (1.8 to 2.1 m) tall

Features: Feathered body, large mothlike wings, giant glowing red eyes

First Sighting: 1966

Range (Area): West Virginia and Ohio

Likes: Flying at top speeds, warning of bad luck

Dislikes: Dogs, cars, humans

THEIR BEGINNINGS

A DEVIL CHILD IS BORN

How did the Jersey Devil come to be? One story tells of a woman from Leeds Point, New Jersey. She gave birth to her thirteenth child. When the baby was born, she cried out, "Let it be the devil!"

She got her wish. The baby turned into a devil. It flew out the chimney and into the woods.

MOTHMAN'S SIMPLE START

Mothman has a simpler story. Two couples were riding in a car one night. They spotted a humanoid figure in the darkness. But it had wings!

The creature stood by the road. Its eyes glowed red. The frightened driver took off fast. But Mothman flew after them. It kept up with the speeding car! Its loud screeches filled the night.

SPOOKY CREATURES

These cryptids have a lot in common. They both enjoy spooking people. They pop up out of nowhere and flash their glowing red eyes. Both have large, fast wings for a quick getaway. They scare drivers on the road at night.

But each has its own odd habits.

FACT
The Jersey Devil has a dark, furry body. Mothman is dark and feathered.

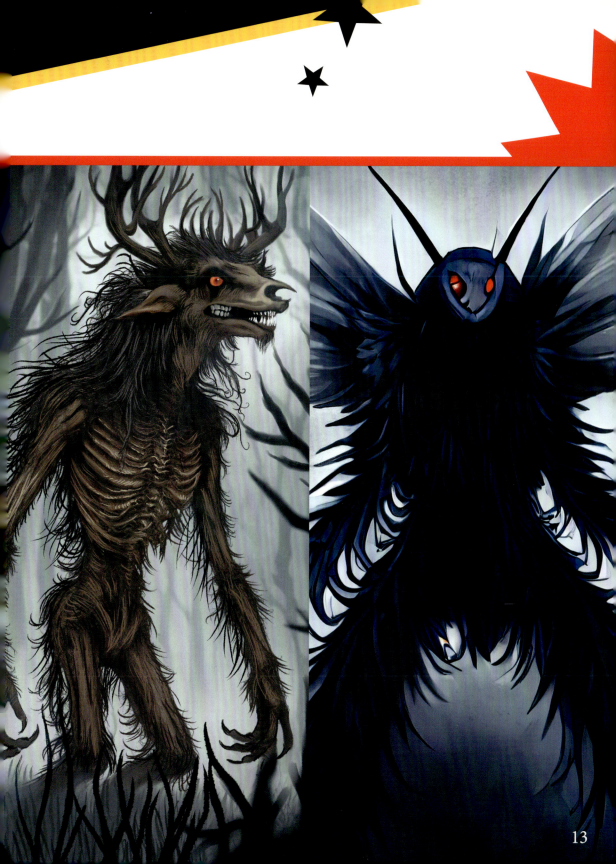

NOW YOU SEE ME, NOW YOU DON'T

Some people think the Jersey Devil is shy. Many have only seen its footprints in the snow. It hides in a pine forest during the day. At night, it lurks outside houses. It does not want to run into anyone.

FACT
The Jersey Devil has also been called Hoodle-Doodle Bird and Wozzle Bug.

CATCH ME IF YOU CAN

Others think the Jersey Devil is not so harmless. It scared many people in the early 1900s. It jumped in front of cars at night. It hovered in the air above people's heads and screeched.

A naval officer once fired cannons at it. Firefighters tried to hose it down. But the Jersey Devil always flew away without a scratch.

A CURSE UPON YOU

The Jersey Devil might put curses on things. It once cursed the weather. Little rainfall led to **drought**. Animals died. Crops stopped growing. Cows would not give milk.

OH NO!

People were scared. They wanted to find the cunning cryptid. Thousands of dollars were offered for its capture. But no one could trap the mysterious Jersey Devil.

RIDE WITH THE WIND

Mothman is not as shy as the Jersey Devil. This cryptid goes after people. It jumps on cars at night and tries to claw its way inside of them. If drivers get away, Mothman chases them.

FACT
Sighting of a flying moth creature were reported in Chicago in 2019.

DOOMSDAY WARNINGS

Some people also say Mothman brings **doom**. In 1967, many people said they spotted it near the Silver Bridge in Ohio. Not long after, the bridge collapsed. Many people died. Had the cryptid brought the **victims** bad luck? Or was it trying to warn people?

THE BATTLE BEGINS

Back to the nighttime battle. The cryptids stare each other down with their glowing red eyes. The Jersey Devil screeches. Just as it looks like it is going to attack, it changes its mind.

It remembers it is shy. It would rather run and hide. The Jersey Devil races into the woods, screeching.

Mothman is startled. It thought the Jersey Devil was going to attack in the air. Time to fly after the scaredy-cat Jersey Devil.

Mothman flies fast through the air, letting out ear-piercing squeaks. It catches up with the Jersey Devil in no time. It wraps its large wings around the scared cryptid.

In a flash, the Jersey Devil bites Mothman with its big teeth. It drives its horns into Mothman's body. Mothman lets out a pained squeak. Too hurt to fight, it flies away fast.

IT'S OVER! THE JERSEY DEVIL WINS!

BUT DO YOU AGREE? Who do you think would win when **the Jersey Devil and Mothman CLASH?**

GLOSSARY

crop (CROP)—a plant grown for profit

cryptid (KRIP-tihd)—a creature whose existence has not been proven

doom (DOOM)—bad luck

drought (DROWT)—a period of dryness due to little rainfall

hind (HIND)—behind or rear

humanoid (HYOO-muh-noyd)—having human features

victim (VIK-tum)—a person who is bothered, hurt, or killed because of a situation or by another person

READ MORE

Anderhagen, Anna. *Chasing the Mothman.* Minneapolis: Abdo Publishing, 2024.

Peterson, Megan Cooley. *The Secret Life of Mothman.* North Mankato, MN: Capstone, 2023.

Stevenson, Paul. *Mysterious Encounters.* Minneapolis: Hungry Tomato, 2025.

INTERNET SITES

Pearson: 10 Creepy Cryptids You Should Know About
pearson.com/languages/en-us/community/blogs/2023/10/english-cryptids.html

Pinelands Preservation Alliance: The Jersey Devil and Folklore
pinelandsalliance.org/learn-about-the-pinelands/pinelands-history-and-culture/the-jersey-devil-and-folklore/

US Ghost Adventures: The True Story Behind the Mothman of West Virginia
usghostadventures.com/haunted-stories/31-days-of-halloween/the-true-story-behind-the-mothman-of-west-virginia/

INDEX

Chicago, IL, 20
curses, 18

drivers, 10, 12, 16, 20

Jersey Devil, The
  attempts to capture, 17, 19
  birth of, 8
  features, 4, 6, 12, 28
  first sighting, 6
  footprints, 14
  height, 6
  nicknames, 6, 14
  range, 6
  shyness, 14

Leeds Point, NJ, 8

Mothman
  features, 4, 7, 10, 12
  first sighting, 7
  flying, 10, 11, 27
  height, 7
  range, 7

Silver Bridge, 22

ABOUT THE AUTHOR

Golriz Golkar is the author of more than 40 nonfiction books for children. Inspired by her work as an elementary school teacher, she loves to write the kinds of books that students are excited to read. Golriz holds a B.A. in American literature and culture from UCLA and an Ed.M. in language and literacy from the Harvard Graduate School of Education. She loves to travel and study languages. Golriz lives in France with her husband and young daughter, Ariane. She thinks children are the very best teachers, and she loves learning from her daughter every day.